Charlie's Spooky Halloween

by
Charles Elias

Charlie's Spooky Halloween
Copyright © 2017 by Charles Elias. All rights reserved.

ISBN: 978-1542986090
Printed in the United States of America.

This book can be purchased on
Amazon.com.

Author resides in Sandown, NH

This story is dedicated to my childhood friends
whom I enjoyed trick-or-treating with in my home town.

Charlie's Spooky Halloween

by
Charles Elias

Early one Saturday morning, Charlie awoke to the sun shining brightly through his bedroom window. As he looked out the window, he noticed a squirrel sitting on a branch gnawing on an acorn. It was autumn and the leaves had changed to yellow, orange, and red. There were many colorful leaves to be seen out of his bedroom window.

Charlie's mom knocked on his bedroom door and said, "Wake up, Charlie. Happy Halloween! Have you thought about what you want to be tonight?"

"I think I will be a pirate," replied Charlie.

"Well, if you want to earn some money for your pirate costume, I will give you five dollars for raking the leaves in front of the house," said his mom.

Charlie quickly jumped out of bed and got dressed.

After Charlie finished his breakfast, he went outside to rake the leaves. There were many leaves that had fallen from the oak and maple trees in front of his house. Charlie raked the front porch and two front yards.

While he was raking, he noticed his friend Joe walking up the street. Charlie shouted out, "Hey, Joe, what are you going to be for Halloween?"

"I am not sure. Maybe I will be a giant Frankenstein," replied Joe. "What are you going to be, Charlie?"

"I have been thinking about being a pirate," replied Charlie. "I am trick-or-treating with John and Alan. Do you want to join us? We are meeting on the corner of Hewlett and Walter Street by the Longfellow School at five o'clock."

Joe replied, "You bet! I will meet you there." Then off Joe went walking up the street to his house, happy to be joining the boys for the big night.

When Charlie finished raking the leaves, he went into the house and asked his mom what was for lunch.

"I made you a peanut butter and jelly sandwich with a glass of fruit punch," replied his Mom. For dessert he had a piece of chocolate cake with a dark chocolate frosting.

When Charlie finished lunch, his mom said, "Here is the five dollars I promised you for doing a great job raking the leaves."

Charlie smiled and could not wait to go shopping in Roslindale Square. The store was a half mile down the street, past the church and the train tracks. After a brisk walk, he arrived at the Five and Dime store. Before looking at the costumes, Charlie walked down the aisle to the back of the store to see the parakeets, turtles, and goldfish. Charlie passed by the model car and airplane kits and headed toward the aisle with a sign that read Halloween Costumes.

Charlie was amazed to see all of the costumes in the Halloween department. Charlie first picked out his pirate's make-up kit with a black patch. He tried a pirate's hat that he found on the top shelf with witch's and cowboy's hats. He picked out a curved silver sword hanging from a hook on the second shelf. Charlie took the sword and tried it on. The sword had a black belt with buckle that wrapped around Charlie's waist. It fit perfectly.

Charlie added up the cost for all of his items. The pirate make-up kit with a black patch cost two dollars. To save money, Charlie decided to purchase a pirate scarf for a dollar and fifty cents instead of the hat. The silver sword cost one dollar and fifty cents. The total came to five dollars, which was the exact amount he had earned that day. As he left the store, Charlie noticed people sitting on stools at the counter. Sam, the chef, was at the grill flipping hamburgers and cooking hot dogs.

Charlie arrived home around four o'clock, just in the nick of time to eat and get ready for Halloween. After dinner, Charlie put on his Halloween costume and walked down the hallway.

Charlie's mom exclaimed, "Charlie, that's a great costume you made for yourself. You look like a real pirate. What do you call yourself?"

"Jean La Foot, gar! " replied Charlie.

"Have fun, but be careful and beware of strangers," said his Mom.

"Okay. See you after trick-or-treating," replied Charlie.

Charlie could not wait to see his friends. It was beginning to get dark. All of sudden, the doorbell rang. Ding dong. Charlie quickly opened the door and was greeted by his friend, John, who was dressed as a ghost, wearing a long white sheet draped over his whole body with two holes for his eyes.

"Great costume," Charlie said.

"Wow you're a real neat pirate. I like the black patch, Charlie," John stated.

"Thanks, John," Charlie replied. "Let's go meet the guys at the corner." Off they went to meet up with Joe and Alan.

Charlie saw Alan and Joe standing at the end of the street. Alan was dressed as a burglar. He was wearing a pair of yellow and black striped pants and shirt with a black mask over his eyes. Joe was standing with Alan, dressed as a giant Frankenstein. He had on a black jacket, black pants, large black shoes, and was wearing a green rubber face mask with green make-up on his hands.

After greeting each other, the boys went from house to house, trick-or-treating and filling their pillow cases with candy. Charlie and his friends walked in and out of houses and ran up and down stairs and stairwells. There were many single family houses and a lot of multi-family homes. Even though it was getting colder, Charlie and the boys continued to march on.

There were groups of kids everywhere wearing different kinds of costumes. Some kids were dressed as superheroes, and some were scary creatures like skeletons and ghouls. This was the most fun Charlie and his friends had had in a long time.

"Let's go to the haunted house in the Arnold Arboretum," said Charlie. The boys had heard stories about an old lady named Mrs. Rex that lived on the hill alone in a haunted house. Some of the boys claimed that she was a scary witch.

They reached a hill with a long stone wall made of granite boulders. Up ahead, there were stone steps that led to a cemetery where there were gravestones with crossbones and skulls dating back to the early 1700's. Charlie, followed by Joe, Alan, and John climbed up the hill.

A full harvest moon with bats flying by could be seen in the distance. The trees cast haunting shadows over the road. The only noise was the sound of the leaves rustling through the cold cemetery, giving an eerie feeling of a spooky Halloween.

As the boys worked their way up the hill, they noticed a dark house with crooked shutters and a long wrap around porch. Standing on the porch was an old lady with white hair and a black scarf wrapped around the top of her head. She was wearing a long flowing dress and pointy black shoes. On the porch were two carved pumpkins with a black cat sitting next to the woman. She was holding a bowl of candy in her hands. Her nose was long and she looked very scary. Was she really a witch, like the witch the boys had spoken about?

Cautiously, the boys walked toward the house and approached Mrs. Rex. The lighting from the jack-o-lanterns shined under the old woman's chin, showing her long scary nose. As the boys approached, she said, "Here, here, boys don't be afraid. Come and get your candy."

Trying to build up courage, Charlie decided to walk up the steps. Frightened, the other boys ran down the hill towards the cemetery. As Charlie walked up the steps with shaky legs, he still had his nerve to say, "Trick or treat." The old woman handed Charlie his candy and some for his friends too.

With a shriek in her voice, Mrs. Rex asked, "Why did your friends run away?"

Charlie said, "I think they were frightened."

After talking to Mrs. Rex, Charlie realized that she was not a scary witch after all. Mrs. Rex had a scratchy voice and a hearing problem. When she leaned over to hear people speak, she appeared scary to them.

Charlie took his white pillow case filled with candy and ran down the hill as fast as he could to catch up to his friends, who were waiting for him at the bottom of the hill. He handed out the candy from Mrs. Rex and explained to them that the old woman was not a scary old witch. After the boys calmed down they headed home, trick or treating along the way.

"See you Monday at school," said Charlie.

Alan and John said good night, and Joe walked up the street to his house. This was a great night with friends.

When Charlie arrived home, he told his mom all about his Halloween adventures with his friends. He said goodnight to his mom and went to bed. As Charlie lay in bed, he realized that old Mrs. Rex was a kind person and that you shouldn't judge a person by the way they looked or sounded.

Made in the USA
San Bernardino,
CA